A PRAYER *for the* EARTH

The Story of Naamah,
Noah's Wife

Sandy Eisenberg Sasso
Illustrated by Bethanne Andersen

A Prayer for the Earth: *The Story of Naamah, Noah's Wife*
Text © 1996 by Sandy Eisenberg Sasso
Illustrations © 1996 by Bethanne Andersen

Library of Congress Cataloging-in-Publication Data
Sasso, Sandy Eisenberg.
  A prayer for the earth : the story of Naamah, Noah's wife / by Sandy Eisenberg Sasso ; illustrated by Bethanne Andersen.
    p.   cm.
  Summary: Noah's wife Naamah is called upon by God to gather the seeds of every type of plant on Earth and bring them safely onto the ark before the great flood.
  ISBN 1-879045-60-5 (hc)
    1. Noah's wife (Biblical figure)—Juvenile fiction. [1. Noah's wife (Biblical figure)—Fiction. 2. Noah's ark—Fiction. 3. Plants—Fiction. 4. Bible stories—O.T.—History of Biblical events—Fiction.] 1. Andersen, Bethanne, 1954–   ill. 11. Title.
PZ7.S24914Pr 1996
[E]—dc20   96-42065

            10 9 8 7 6 5 4 3 2 1
ISBN 1-879045-60-5 (Hardcover)
Manufactured in the United States of America

Book and jacket designed by Delphine Keim Campbell

A portion of all sales of *A Prayer for the Earth* is donated by the publisher to groups working to preserve our environment.

For People of All Faiths, All Backgrounds
JEWISH LIGHTS Publishing
A Division of LongHill Partners, Inc.
P.O. Box 237
Sunset Farm Offices, Rte. 4
Woodstock, Vermont 05091
Tel: (802) 457-4000   Fax: (802) 457-4004

In memory of my father
Israel Eisenberg
who planted my childhood garden

—S.E.S.

To Tye and Chase,
who have made
walking on this earth a joy

—B.A.

I am grateful to Alan Kapuler and Andrew Schulman for their botanical expertise and love of nature which helped this book to grow.

—S.E.S.

Naamah was

Noah's wife,

and why was

she called Naamah?

Because her

deeds were

neimim (pleasing).

— *Bereshit Rabba 23:3*

In the time when the world was still young, plants and animals and people filled all creation. But the people were not always kind to one another. God was sad for the ruin which people had brought to the garden called earth.

In earth's garden, there lived a man named Noah and a woman named Naamah. Noah and Naamah were kind and loving and walked in God's ways.

God said to Noah and Naamah, "I have seen great wickedness on the earth. There is too much hate in people's hearts. But your hearts are good, and you can help me begin again."

God said to Noah, "Make yourself an ark of gopher wood. Build it three floors high with many rooms and cover it with pitch. Put a window in the ark for light. Do this quickly, for I am about to bring a great flood to destroy all that is under the sky. Bring two of every animal that lives on this earth, birds and cattle and creeping things of every kind. Gather enough food for you and for them and store it in the ark."

Noah did as God commanded.

Then God called out to Naamah, "Walk across the land and gather the seeds of all the flowers and all the trees. Take two of every kind of living plant and bring each one onto the ark. They shall not be for food, but they shall be your garden, to tend and to keep. Work quickly. The rains begin tomorrow."

Naamah tied an apron of many pockets around her waist and walked through all the earth's fields and gardens. Her legs grew strong and her feet were as the wings of birds, so she traveled far and never grew tired.

Naamah did as God commanded.

She journeyed into the forest and carefully gathered the spores from the moss that made a carpet at her feet. She placed them in the cool deep pockets of her apron, away from the light of the sun.

She came upon the giant redwoods. They carried their cones too high for her hands to reach. "God," called Naamah, "blow me a wind so that the redwoods will let go of their seeds and I may gather them."

Just then a fierce howling sound blew through the forest. Branches trembled and the wind stirred the ground. The air became dark with the dust of the earth. Naamah grabbed hold of a tree trunk so she would not be swept away. Then just as suddenly as the storm began, the wind grew calm. There at Naamah's feet were the cones of the redwoods.

Naamah picked acorns from the oak trees, and nuts from the pecan and pistachio. The winged seeds of the maples snapped under the gentle pull of her hands. She carefully lifted the seedlings of the cedar and cypress, the persimmon and plum. She found every tree, from acacia to ziziphus.

Naamah walked into the fields right past the dandelions, pretending not to notice their feathery yellow heads sprouting over the grass. "Naamah," called God, "gather seeds of *every* living plant!" And Naamah knew that God meant the dandelions too. Reluctantly, she placed their seeds in her pockets with all the others. Because Naamah had ignored them, God made certain that dandelions would cover the earth.

Naamah gathered the seeds of the sunflowers and buttercups, the orchids and jasmine. The fields blossomed with dahlias and daffodils, lilies and lavender. She picked two of every kind and planted them in red clay pots to carry onto the ark. She collected all the flowers, from the amaryllis to the zinnia.

Tomatoes burst with seed and avocado pits rested in their green fruit. The fields were ripe with potatoes and pomegranates, oranges and okra, lima beans and lemons. Naamah carried large straw baskets to hold all the varieties of fruits and vegetables, everything from apples to zucchini.

When Naamah had collected the seeds and seedlings of every living plant upon the earth, she brought them onto the ark. In the center of the ark she swept away some of the hay that covered the floor, and she made a space for all her plants.

She carefully arranged them into groups and families. The garbanzos, peas and soybeans belonged in the family of legumes. Among the herbs she gathered oregano, rosemary and thyme. Wheat, rice and barley were

in the family of grasses. The citruses boasted oranges, grapefruits and tangerines. Among the family of lilies sprouted onions, chives and tulips.

Naamah arranged every plant and seed, each in its special place on the ark. Then she made a sign that read:

NAAMAH'S GARDEN——these plants are not for food.

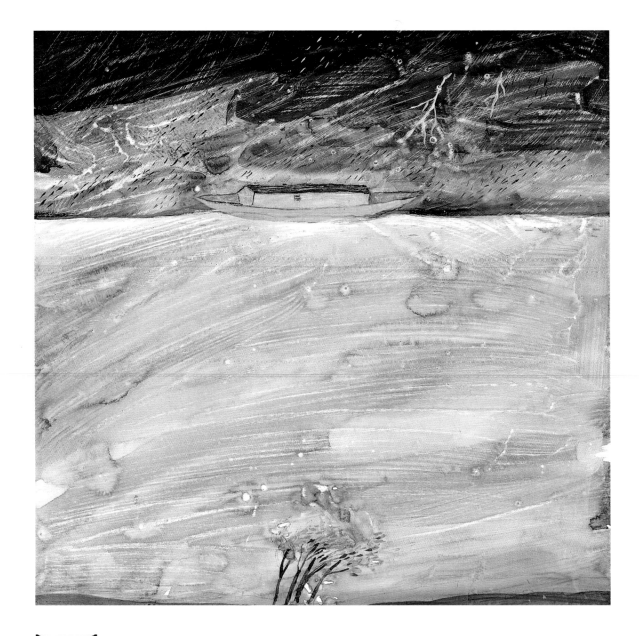

T hen the sun disappeared, lightning flashed and thunder boomed. Dark clouds filled the sky and rain poured from the heavens until the waters covered all the lime green aspens and the emerald green pines.

Noah and Naamah looked out over the waters and were sad for all that had been destroyed. For forty days and forty nights the skies never brightened, and the rains never ceased.

On the ark Noah and Naamah cared for the lions and leopards, the

porcupines and parrots, the opossums and orangutans. Some of the animals liked to eat in the day, and others wanted to eat at night. Just as the squirrels closed their eyes for the evening, the owls hooted for food.

There were as many sounds as there were animals on the ark. The coyotes howled, the snakes hissed and the peacocks shrieked; the noise never stopped. Water was everywhere, but there was none for a bath. The smell of the animals filled the ark.

Noah and Naamah's problems worsened when the waters began to toss and turn and the ark rocked from side to side. The animals were thrown about like a bunch of loose marbles. Their stomachs fluttered like the wings of a hundred butterflies. Even the bright yellow mane of the lion turned green.

At these times Noah and Naamah would breathe the sweet aroma of the flowers and sit in the quiet of the plants that they called Naamah's garden. They prayed for the rains to stop.

After forty days and forty nights, a rushing wind rolled over the waters and the rains ceased. The ark rested on the mountains of Ararat. When Naamah and Noah looked out the window atop the ark, they saw the black sky soften into shades of blue. Noah decided to send a raven from the ark to scout for dry land. But the raven was not happy to leave the ark.

"Why choose me as your messenger?" cawed the raven. "I gave you no more trouble than any of the other birds. Who knows what waits for me outside the ark! Perhaps it is so cold or so hot that I will die and

nevermore will there be ravens on the earth."

Naamah held the raven in her hands and whispered to him, "Do not be afraid. It is God who has chosen you to be a messenger. Take this olive seed and when you see even a small patch of dry land, let it fall to the earth."

The raven felt comforted by Naamah's gentle words. When Noah sent him from the ark, he carried the olive seed in his beak. He flew back and forth until he finally dropped the olive seed on a tiny patch of land barely visible above the water. Then he flew back to the ark.

Then Noah sent out a dove to see if the waters had decreased. But the waters still covered the earth and the dove returned to the ark. After many days, Noah sent out the dove for a second time. Naamah whispered to the dove, "Bring us back an olive branch that has grown from the seed the raven has planted." And the dove flew over the waters, its wings casting a moving shadow over the seas.

In a few days the dove returned. Just as Naamah had hoped, the dove carried an olive branch in her beak. "Dry land!" shouted Noah. "God has plantcd an olive tree for us!" Naamah just smiled.

The dove went out once again, and this time it did not return. Finally the ground was dry and firm. Two by two, Noah led the animals from the ark. Some pranced, some flew, some slithered, and in this way they spread out over the earth.

Naamah carefully placed all the seeds and seedlings in the deep pockets of her apron. As soon as she set foot on the new land, Naamah knelt down, put her hands into the soft moist earth, and made small cradles in which to plant. She placed downy tufts of milkweed seeds in her palms and held them up to the sky to let the wind carry them in all directions.

aamah took off her sandals and let her feet sink into the soft soil. She sighed with delight at the touch of the land. Morning gave way to afternoon, and Naamah worked without rest. As she patted the earth around a small raspberry bush, a dark red berry fell generously into her hand. The taste of ripened raspberry refreshed her.

God saw all that Naamah had planted and God said, "Because of your great love for the earth, I will make you guardian of all living plants, and I will call you Emzerah, Mother of Seed." For a single moment, God gave Naamah's eyes the vision to see into the future and from one end of the earth to the other. She saw how the seeds were carried great distances, and how they landed safely on the soft ground. As God had promised, the dandelions were everywhere.

Naamah delighted in how the trees grew tall and spread umbrellas of shade over the earth. Flowers sprinkled yellow, peach and lilac over the fields.

Naamah was pleased to be surrounded by all the living plants, even the dandelions. She lay down in a grassy meadow and with each deep breath she smelled lilies, lavender and mint. A gentle wind blew through the grasses, and it sounded as if the meadow was whispering a prayer.

Naamah slept in the quiet of growing things.

G od was pleased with Naamah's work. To this day whenever someone digs in the earth and plants a seed, God remembers the Mother of Seed and Naamah's garden continues to grow.